Books in the Linkers series

Homes discovered through Art & Technology
Homes discovered through Geography
Homes discovered through History
Homes discovered through Science

Toys discovered through Art & Technology
Toys discovered through Geography
Toys discovered through History
Toys discovered through Science

Myself discovered through Art & Technology
Myself discovered through Geography
Myself discovered through History
Myself discovered through Science

Water discovered through Art & Technology
Water discovered through Geography
Water discovered through History
Water discovered through Science

Reprinted 2001
First paperback edition 1996
First published 1996 in hardback by A&C Black (Publishers) Limited
37 Soho Square, London W1D 3QZ

ISBN 0-7136-4601-2
A CIP catalogue record for this book is available from the British Library.

Commissioned photographs by Zul Mukhida
Design by Jean Wheeler

Consultant: Hazel Grice

Acknowledgements

The publishers would like to thank the following organizations for supplying some of the toys used in this book: The Early Learning Centre, Swindon; 3 (top), 5 (right), 10 (both), 11, 16 (both), 17 (both), 18 (recorder and bells), 20 (bottom), 21, Gamleys Ltd; cover, 2, 3 (bottom), 4 (both), 6, 7 (both), 12, 13 (top), 14, 15 (both), 18 (drum), 19 (top).

Printed and bound in Italy by L.E.G.O.

Toys

discovered through

Science

Karen Bryant-Mole

Contents

A & C Black • London

Your toys

You probably play with toys every day. But do you ever stop and wonder how your toys work?

What makes a bicycle move along?

What makes these train carriages
stay together?

How does this torch work?

All of these questions, and more, will
be answered in this book.

Push and Pull

Lots of toys have wheels.
Wheels help toys to move along
smoothly and easily.

Moving

This pram has wheels but it is not moving.
It needs something to make it start moving.

Push

What the pram needs
is a push.
If you want the pram
to keep moving you
have to keep pushing.

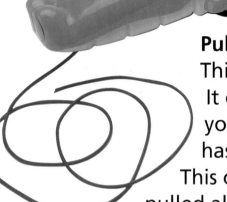

Pull

This toy has wheels, too. It could be pushed, but if you look you will see that it has some string tied to it. This crocodile is meant to be pulled along.

All toys with wheels need something to make them go. Pushing and pulling are two ways of doing this.
Can you think of some more toys that can be pushed or pulled?

Body power

We can use different parts of our bodies to make things move.

Sit-on toys
Lots of young children have sit-on toys like this. To make the toy move you have to put your feet on the ground and use your feet and legs to push the car forward.

Bikes

The girl on this bike is using her feet
to make the pedals go round.
As they go round they make a chain turn.
The chain makes the back wheel go round
which moves the bike along.

Fast feet

Roller boots cannot move by
themselves but once your feet are
strapped in and you move your legs,
they can carry you along very quickly.

Storing energy

Twisting

The boy in the picture below has twisted the swing round and round. Can you see all the twists in the ropes? Do you know what will happen when he lifts his feet off the ground?

Spinning

As the ropes unwind, the boy spins round and round.
Twisting stores up energy.
As the ropes untwist, the energy is released.
Energy can be used in different ways to make things move.

Rubber bands

This flying elephant is powered by a rubber band!
When the propellor is turned, it winds up
the rubber band.
When the elephant is thrown,
the rubber band unwinds
and helps to send the
elephant soaring
through the air.

Rubber bands are good for
storing energy because they are stretchy.
A stretchy rubber band can store more energy
than something that does not stretch.

Clockwork

Clockwork toys work by storing energy, too.

Key

When the key on the side of this helicopter is turned, it winds up a piece of machinery inside. The piece of machinery is called a clockwork mechanism.

Wind it up

If you look carefully, you might be able to see a thin, flat piece of metal wound round into a coil. As the key is turned it winds up the metal coil.

When the coil unwinds it turns a set of wheels called cogs.

The last cog makes the helicopter move.

Turning and pulling

Clockwork toys are not always wound up by turning a key.
Some have a knob that can be turned.

Others, like this rabbit, are wound up by pulling a piece of string.

Although rubber bands and clockwork both store energy, clockwork is used more often in toys.

This is because something made from metal is less likely to break than something made from rubber.

Batteries

Lots of toys are powered by batteries. Unlike rubber bands and clockwork, batteries already have energy stored inside them, waiting to be used.

Radio

This radio is powered by batteries. When it is switched on, the energy that is stored in the batteries makes the radio work.

FM
88 94 98 102 105 108

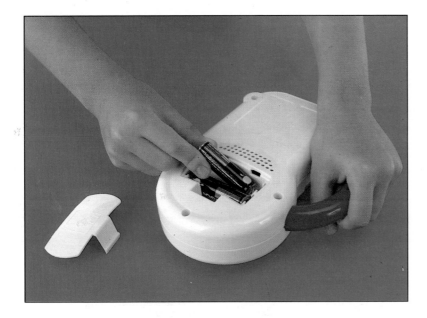

Circuits

When the batteries are put into the radio they become part of a loop, called a circuit.
The energy from the batteries can flow around this circuit.

On and off

Most toys that are powered by batteries have a switch that turns them on and off.
There is a yellow switch on this walkie talkie.
Switches usually move a piece of metal inside the toy.
This completes or breaks the circuit and turns the toy on or off.

Light

Some battery toys use the energy in the battery to power light bulbs.

Torches

The light bulb in this torch has become part of the circuit.

When the switch is turned on, and the circuit is completed, the energy flows through a thin wire in the light bulb, called a filament.
This makes the bulb light up.

Filters

Most light bulbs are clear and give off a white light.

The colour of the light can be changed by using thin sheets of coloured plastic, called filters.

To change the colour of the light beam, the filter has to be moved across in front of the light bulb. This torch has a green filter and a red filter.

Pictures

Lights can even be used to make pictures.

With this toy, you press the spots you want to use and then watch your design light up.

Magnets

When this train is pulled along the track, the carriages stay joined together.
They are not clipped or hooked to each other.
Magnets keep them together.

What is a magnet?
A magnet is a special piece of metal that other magnets and some other metals cling to.

There is a small magnet on each end of the train's carriages. The magnetism is strong enough to keep the carriages together when the train is pulled along.

Fishing game

Magnets are used in this fishing game. There is a magnet on the end of each fishing rod and a piece of metal on each fish.

When a player catches a fish, the metal on the fish clings to the magnet on the fishing rod.
The fish can then be pulled out.

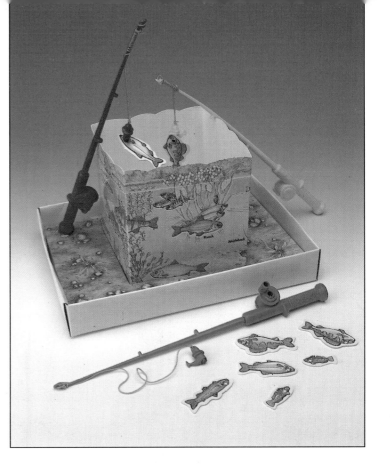

Travel games

Travel games often have magnetic playing pieces.
Magnetism stops the noughts and crosses falling off this board.

Sound

When you were a baby, one of your first toys was probably a rattle. A rattle makes a noise.
Babies love toys that make sounds.

Noisy toys
Sounds can be made in lots of different ways.

Have a look at these noisy toys. Can you see one that is blown, one that is shaken and one that is hit?

Fire engine

This fire engine makes a wailing sound as it travels along. It sounds like a real fire engine.

Tape recorders

A tape recorder plays tapes for us to listen to.
Tape recorders also let us record our own sounds onto tapes.

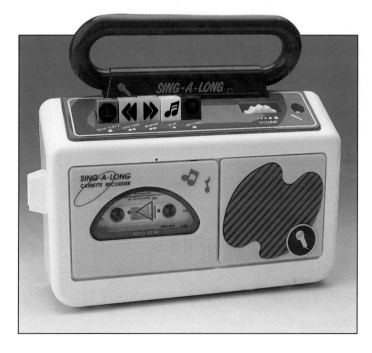

Some toys make loud sounds.
Some make quiet sounds.
Other toys let you decide how loud you want the sound to be.

Floating toys

Some toys are meant to be played with in water.

Bobbing boats
You could push this toy along but it is more fun to play with it in the bath.
It floats in the water and will bob around as you move about.

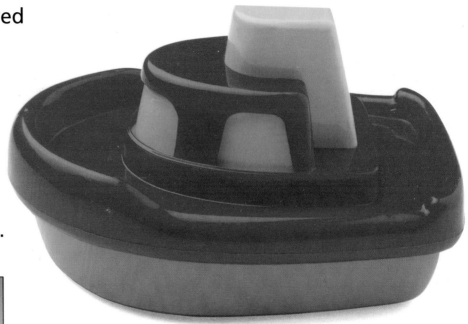

Hollow toys
Lots of floating toys are hollow.
Toys like this, that have air trapped inside them, usually make very good water toys.

Plastic

Many water toys are made from plastic.

Most metals go rusty if they keep getting wet, but plastic will not go rusty.

Plastic is also waterproof. This means that, unlike paper or cardboard, water cannot soak into it.

Changing shapes

Most of the toys you play with
stay the same shape.
But you can change the shape
of some toys.

Play dough
Have you ever played with
play dough?
You can squeeze and press
it into all sorts of shapes.

When you have finished
playing, you can store the
dough in a container until the
next time you want to use it.
Play dough can be squashed
and twisted and rolled,
over and over again.

Clay

Clay can be squashed, twisted
and made into different shapes, too.
Then it can be left to dry out.
When the clay has dried out, its shape
cannot be changed again.

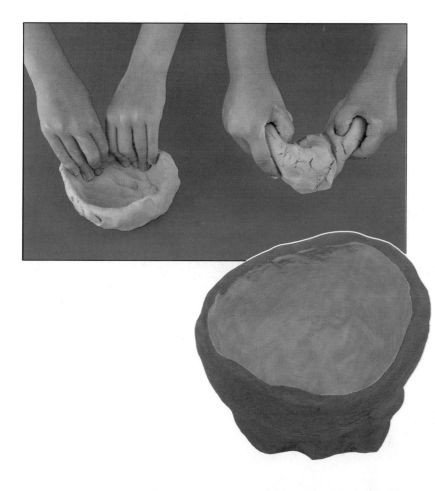

These things have been made from
clay which has been left to dry and
then painted.

Glossary

circuit a loop through which electricity can flow

cogs a set of notched wheels that connect together

coil wound round and round to form a circle shape

design pattern or picture

energy the power needed to make something work or move

filament very thin wire in a light bulb that heats up when electricity passes through it and glows with a white light

hollow with nothing but air inside

mechanism a set of parts in a machine

propellor blades that turn to make some boats and planes move

Index

How to use this book

This book takes a familiar topic and focuses on one area of the curriculum: science.
The book is intended as a starting point, illustrating one of the many different angles from which a topic can be studied.

It should act as a springboard for further investigation, activity or information seeking.

The following list of books may prove useful.

Further books to read

Series	Title	Author	Publisher
	First Book of Science	G. Waters	Usborne
Science Activities	Science with Batteries	P. Shipton	
	Science with Magnets	H. Edom	
	Science with Light & Mirrors	"	
Simple Science	My magnet	Robert Pressling	A&C Black
	My boat	Kay Davies &	
	My car	Wendy Oldfield	
	My balloon	" "	
Starting Out	Games and Toys		Heinemann
Toppers	Living with Light	Nicola Baxter	Watts
Toybox Science	All titles	Chris Ollerenshaw &	A&C Black
		Wendy Oldfield	
What do ... do?	Screws	David Glover	Heinemann
	Springs	"	
	Slopes and Wedges	"	
	Levers	"	
	Wheels and Cranks	"	
	Pulleys and Gears	"